Inside The Wire

by

Elizabeth Mawer

Bloomington, IN

authorHOUSE™

Milton Keynes, UK

AuthorHouse™
1663 Liberty Drive, Suite 200
Bloomington, IN 47403
www.authorhouse.com
Phone: 1-800-839-8640

AuthorHouse™ UK Ltd.
500 Avebury Boulevard
Central Milton Keynes, MK9 2BE
www.authorhouse.co.uk
Phone: 08001974150

This book is a work of non-fiction. Unless otherwise noted, the author
and the publisher make no explicit guarantees as to the accuracy
of the information contained in this book and in some cases, names
of people and places have been altered to protect their privacy.

First published by AuthorHouse 5/18/2006

ISBN: 1-4259-3598-2 (sc)

Printed in the United States of America
Bloomington, Indiana

This book is printed on acid-free paper.

This book is dedicated to four, very dear and sincere friends, all of whom, without there continued support, care and love, I'm certain I would not be here today. Also to my friend's son, who took on so much for someone so young.

It acknowledges, on my behalf, if no-one else's that Racism, Harassment, Intimidation and Bullying exist within our Prison system. Although others would have you believe different.

The Prison Service, in general is depicted in "a bad light", mostly by people who do not understand it and what it is, we try to achieve.

This is my story – I leave it to you too decide.

"The Grange"

I joined the Prison Service in 1990, after leaving Her Majesties Forces. As with most jobs these days you have to complete an induction period of two weeks. My Induction was to be at "The Grange" and it was as its name suggested a "Grange". A grand old house with a built in swimming pool, a grand entrance hall and superb grounds.

I was to spend two weeks here, learning all about prison life. It was to be a scary fortnight as I did not know what to expect. The officers were nice but cold. Myself and two other colleagues I joined with were classed as "Outsiders" and were kept very much out of things. At times you felt like you dare not talk to anyone (staff) and if you did, you were given the "Evil eye"- usually by some ones girl friend.

I was met on my first day by a young blonde Senior Officer who firmly told us what we could expect over the next two weeks. The following day I asked her if it was possible to have Christmas Day off. Not an unreasonable request I thought as we were only there to observe. I was firmly put in my place and told that if they all had to work then so should I.

My request was denied. I remember thinking that I hoped that not all Senior Officers were like her.

I met that lady again socially some six years later. We have remained good friends ever since, so much so that she is one of a few colleagues that kept me strong and focused during my ordeal with the Prison Service and HMP Sutton a few years later.

She is held in the highest of regard, not only by the service as a manager but by me as a very dear and sincere friend.

My two weeks at the grange were quite uneventful, one day being very much the same as another. Getting up, going to the gym for a beasting, watching prisoners, answering questions and then onto the pub. Day in day out. All that could be said is that it had a very good pub at the end of the road.

I was pleased to leave the Grange and move onto the Training College, where I hoped this would prepare me more for what was to come.

I don't know what became of my two colleagues, I never saw them again. I was told some years later that one of them had to resign due to inappropriate relations with an offender. True or not I don't know.

There's a saying within the system, that if you want to know what's happening – ask a prisoner as they usually seem to know everything before the staff do, and its true. But I never did ask!

College –
What Not to Do

My next journey took me to the training college at Newbold Revell. One hell of a place to try and find. It is a very impressive building, with its own gym, chapel and a very nice lake at the rear.

You had your own room with a bed, TV, drink making facilities and a wash basin. The wash basins were hardly ever used as they were notorious for being urinated in by the male staff that were there on courses. (Sorry guys, but you do have some disgusting habits).

The training itself lasted twelve weeks. We were taught on radio procedures, Health and Safety issues, Control and Restraint (more commonly know as C&R, or wrapping people up). The 101 different types of forms and paperwork and Race Relations.

Only in years to come would I accept and admit that the Prison Service has serving officers of all ranks that are openly racist. This all goes against the Home Office policy on Racial Discrimination and behaviour.To tackle a problem you have to admit that there is one. I found that issues on Racism were very much "swept under the carpet", therefore No issue and No problem.

The Control and Restraint side of the training was very good. However at times you had a number of guys that had to prove how strong they were, how easily they could break your arm or injure your neck. The injuries that were substained at the college were tremendous, considering its all about using minimum force. This behaviour was highlighted many times throughout my career, not only by male staff but females as well.Whilst training we had to endure lots of role play sessions in C&R. On one occasion during a fight in a cell, we were all kitted out in riot gear (helmet, overalls, gloves and knee pads). I grabbed hold of a pair of legs that were kicking about all over the place. I naturally thought they belonged to the prisoner. It wasn't until we had finished that I found out that I had actually held onto the legs of one of the officers. I fell about laughing and so did everyone else. Luckily for me this never happened in real life. I blamed it on the helmet. It was two sizes to big and I had to pad it out with newspaper. Then when I put the visor down you became so steamed up because of your breathing that you couldn't see anything anyway.

Apart from a few exams that you had to study for, most of which were not that hard, most of your time was spent propping up the bar and in some cases "bed hopping", which would happen a lot more that some would like it to be known, especially with the instructors, but did this stop them – Of course it didn't. Although to be fair there were some students and Instructors with morals!

Training, was described by many as "Death by overhead projector" by instructors with bad breath and an ego problem.

At about the Ten Week point, we had to make three choices of where we would like to be posted after leaving training. Obviously we all wanted to go somewhere near home, wherever that may be. Some trainers told you to be honest about your choice as you would probably get what you asked for. Others said "If you want to go up north, choose a prison in the south and vice versa, as you won't get what you ask for".In the end you were so confused you didn't know what to do for the best.

I was so confused I chose a Prison in Lincolnshire and two prisons in the North of England. I thought I would be bound to get one of them.

A week later we received our letters stating where we were to be posted. Mine said "Bullfield Hall". Bullfield Hall I thought where the hell is that, I had never heard of the place.I suppose I was just relieved that it wasn't the notorious "Holloway".
Holloway had a reputation that was in a league of its own. Oh well Bullfield Hall it was.

We had a great passing out parade. We were now fully pledged Prison Officers.I was taught everything I needed to know, but in reality new absolutely nothing.

Sunny Essex

I turned up at Bullfield Hall at 9.00am sharp, as instructed in full No1 uniform, with hat in tow. I remember seeing an officer walking to her car, she was overweight and scruffy. Apparently she had just finished her night shift. I remember thinking "what the hell have I joined".Once I had entered the main gate, it was firmly slammed behind me. A voice shouted at me from somewhere "you can get that bloody hat off to start with". Then a body appeared from a door way. She was a Senior Officer and angry looking. By this stage I was beginning to dislike Senior Officers.

"I suppose you're the new trainee" she shouted. I didn't know whether to answer or run like hell.Almost straight away I was assigned to another officer who I would follow around everywhere for the next three weeks, her knick name was "Acky". She was great; she had been in the service for some years. She was tuff, supportive, sensitive and when times permitted very funny. Acky was "my rock" for the seven years I was to spend at Bullfield Hall.

Bullfield was a purpose built prison, very cold and drab. The name Bullfield came from the building next door. In its hay day it would have been a magnificent building, now it was a run down mansion with no central heating and a leaking roof. Although the Home Office did allow us to use it as our social club, which was ok in the summer but cold and damp in the winter. It served its purpose and we had some great parties.

After six months my probation period had ended, without I may add of anyone informing me of the fact and I could now be in-charge of a wing and junior staff.

One day whilst working down the segregation unit, I had to let a young prisoner out for her daily exercise. Her name was Karen, she was very loud and abusive and very demanding. We never had problems letting them out, only trying to get them back in again. Karen would walk around the yard, which had a 15ft brick wall around it and razor wire on the top. She would be muttering to herself, stopping occasionally at the office window to hurl abuse at the staff. After five minutes had passed we realised that it had gone very quiet and we couldn't see Karen through the window. We assumed that she must have been stood in the door way leading onto the yard. But as we were always told not to assume anything, we decided to go and look. As we turned the corner to the corridor, she was nowhere to be seen. At that point we both turned to each other and said "No". We opened the gate leading onto the yard, looked around and then gazed up at the roof. Karen had climbed up through the razor wire and was trying to pull herself onto the roof. As my colleague radioed for assistance, I decided to go up after Karen. After being cut quite badly by the wire I decided to climb back down. By now Karen had made it onto the roof. When she started out she was wearing jogging bottoms and a top. By the time she had made it through the wire, all her clothes had been torn away; she ended up wearing only a pair of knickers and a bra. Within seconds staff had arrived with a ladder. Acky had climbed onto the roof trying to persuade Karen to come down. But all Karen kept shouting was "If you come near me im going to jump". Obviously this was not something we wanted to happen. Fifteen or twenty minutes went by and we were still trying to talk her down and Karen was still saying that she would jump, when a voice shouted from a near by window

"Then fucking jump and give us all a rest". Everyone just burst into laughter including Karen who promptly came down. So thank you to whoever you were that shouted those kind words of advice to a fellow prisoner.

I was happy and enjoying my new job. One day I decided to give up smoking. I knew there was a good chance that I might become a littler ratty, so I told all of the prisoners on my unit and strangely enough I had the support of all of them. They were in large a good bunch of girls. The first day didn't go to bad, but I had underestimated how much time I spent around smokers. As time went on it was noticeable that I was becoming irritable and snappy. On or around the fourth day I snapped. I kicked a bucket out of the wing office onto the landing, narrowingly missing some ones head. Slamming everything in my path. Then an elderly prisoner came up to me and said " Here, it's a roll up I know, its all ive got, for fuck sake smoke it miss and give us all a rest". I did smoke it, thinking only afterwards that I hoped it wasn't a joint, but it wasn't and I dually replaced it.

One noticeable difference I found straight away between the male and female estates (Prisons) is that females seem to be on a lot more medication than the male prisoners. At Bellfield, medication was given out three times a day. There were some girls that seemed to be "Drugged up" continuously throughout the day. If the nurses had a particular prisoner that was causing them problems, they would give her liquid paracetomol and say to the woman that it was something else. It never hurt them but it was a way of getting rid of them. Some girls never knew any difference. On one particular occasion (I can't remember why), the nurse came onto the wing with the drugs trolley. I would have estimated that out of thirty or so women, twenty of them would have been on some kind of medication. Unbeknown to the staff the prisoners were going to storm the drugs trolley and over power the staff. (There were only three of us and one of them was a nurse). All this happened within fifteen seconds or so, we never knew what hit us. Needless to say the drugs trolley never came onto the wings again. Luckily no harm came to any of the prisoners or the staff. One thing was very noticeable about Bellfield and the staff. If there was an incident, the staff, once there shift had finished would go to the pub and discuss any problems, we would always make sure we were all ok. If we needed to talk, then that was the time to do it. We kept this rule because a lot of us lived on our own and the last thing you needed was to go home alone and dwell on what had happened. That only made the situation look a lot worse.

I used to work on a wing that was the furthest away from the corridor where Miss Jenkins used to sit and do the detailing of staff. She was a funny, quite old Principle officer who did nothing all day but work out who was going to be on shift months ahead. One day, whilst sat in my office, the telephone rang, it was miss Jenkins, she asked if I could come down to her office. "Sure" I said, ill be there in a few minutes. I had to lock away what few girls I had out on the wing then went down to see her. I stood there waiting; you never interrupted Miss Jenkins when she was working. Her mind was like a well hot coiled spring. "Just get me the detail of the wall, would you please". "Of course" I replied. I handed it to her and carried on standing there thinking she will tell me what she's called me down for in a minute. "That's it, that's all I wanted" she said. You soon got to know that Miss Jenkins never got up out of her seat for anything if she could help it. Miss Jenkins knew everyone from the way in which they rattled there keys and the sound there shoes made as you walked past her door. She never looked up. But she knew who you were. She was an excellent detailing officer, if you ever wanted time off, she would either say yes or no straight away. If it was yes, you were sorted. If it was no, then you knew there was no chance. What you didn't realise was that she would phone around the other staff, saying "Can you work this for me and I will give you that day off. What she was really trying to do was to make sure you got the leave you wanted. All the staff knew this, so Miss Jenkins was one person you never said no to, every time she asked you to extend your shift or come into work on your day off you would because you always knew she would go that extra mile for you when you needed it. In all the seven years I knew her, Miss Jenkins could never remember people's names. It was always err Miss, err Officer. She was so funny.

When its time to lock the girls away for the evening, they are given five minute to collect there hot water, use the toilet and say good night to there mates. You then hear an almighty shout from the officer in charge of the wing "Time ladies, behind your own doors". Then for the next five minutes is what can only be described as chaos starts. The women start screaming, kissing and hugging there mates (Again), running up and down the stairs and across the landings. Mean while the staff are starting to lock any women that are in there cells away for the evening.

Each prison is different, but at Bullfield if a woman was not in her cell by the time you get there, then you would lock the cell door. The prisoner is then placed on report and in front of the governor the following morning. When the prisoner finally arrives you have to unlock the cell only to re-lock it again with her inside.

Prisoners are placed on report when they disobey the rules, this happened everyday at Bullfield.

Mornings was the worst part of the day for staff. Especially back in the early 90's.

The woman had no access to toilets throughout the night, if they needed to go then they had to use a potty. Which meant that when we unlocked the doors in the morning you had around 30 potty's waiting to be emptied down the sluice. The stench was unbelievable at times.

I had been ordered on day to place an elderly African woman on report for repeatedly emptying the contents of her pot down the kitchen sink.(Needless to say that a lot of the time the pot contained stools). On the adjudication, I read out my report to the Governor. When I had finished reading it the governor asked me for the evidence. Evidence I thought – did she really think I was going to pick up the stools and place them in an evidence bag. I think not some how.

For a year and a half I worked in the prison canteen, which is basically a shop where the prisoners can by toiletries, tobacco, food and stamps. The women could spend there wages in the shop once a week. On a Monday morning they could put in a fruit order. I would go into town and buy whatever they ordered providing they could afford it. On particular Monday an Afro-Caribbean woman put in an order for bananas. This was not a problem, I purchased them and on my return to the prison had them delivered to the wing. About 15minutes later I received a call from the wing officer asking if I could attend the wing to sort out a problem with the fruit order. On entering the wing a prisoner came up to me shouting abuse and saying "What the fuck am I supposed to do with these", "Eat them" I said, "I know there a little small, but there really tasty". The prisoner looked at me, I thought at one point she was going to smack me, but she turned away muttering something to herself. Two young prisoners were stood nearby; they were in fits of laughter. I remember saying to them "You just can't please some people". I turned and walked into the wing office. About 2-3 minutes later one of the youngsters that was stood near me called me from the landing and asked if she could show me something. I met her on the upper landing and she led me to a cell. She told me to look through the observation flap, with that she turned and walked away. As I opened the flap, I found the afro Caribbean woman having what can only be described as sex with a banana. (At this point I will leave it to your imagination). I turned and walked away thinking thank god no one could see the expression on my face, little did I know that the young prisoner had been watching me all of the time and then dually told the rest of her mates. I never bought small bananas again – for anyone!.

Every so often you would have to work a week of night shifts, which wasn't bad because it meant that you had a week off afterwards. The only problem doing nights at Bullfield was it meant you had to patrol the segregation unit (The block). It was a very dark and very cold even in the summer and it always smelt of pipe tobacco. Some staff used to say it was George our resident ghost. He apparently used to be the gardener and died somewhere near where the block was built. We used to scare ourselves that much that very often we would go round in pairs.

During my time at Bullfield, I spent many months running "F" wing, which was sadly named by staff as the "Muppet" wing, as the majority of the prisoners on this unit had either physical and or mental psychological problems.

In the 90's it was acceptable to interact with the prisoners on evening association (playing cards, pool, and chess).

One night on evening association I was playing draughts with a young girl called Wendy, she was generally no problem, but she did have a speech problem and was deaf in both ears..During our game a girl called Karen (Yes the same one who climbed up onto the roof threw the razor wire) kept pestering me for my attention. She didn't want anything in particular, she was just bored. When she finally walked away I muttered to myself "I wish someone would shut her up". Between games, Wendy and I both went to make a hot drink. We returned to our table some ten minutes later. I had just sat down to play another game when Karen came up to me and said that Wendy had assaulted her. She demanded I place her on report and take her to the block. I walked into the office with the intention of talking to Karen, who by now had followed me in. Before I could say anything Karen had grabbed the HiFi unit of the wall and threw it at me. Also in the wing office was another officer of some 50yrs +. Although she was quite capable of handling herself, the younger members of staff always looked out for her, it was the thing to do. Anyway, by trying to stop the hifi system from hitting me too hard, I fell over onto a radiator hitting my head. Whilst concussed and two broken ribs a fight broke out. I remember shouting "Some one press the alarm bell". Luckily some one did, she was called Mama. (Although not politically correct these days) that was what she was known as. Mama tried to grab Karen off me just as the staff arrived. The staff mistakenly thought Mama was part of the problem and they tried to C&R her, until I shouted out that she was helping and to let her go. Karen was taken away to the Block. My fault you might say, and yes I would agree with you. From that day on I learnt to keep my opinions to myself especially around deaf people with selected hearing. My thanks go out to Mama, who, had she not have pressed the alarm bell, then my injuries would certainly have been a lots worse, so thanks Mama.

College prepared us for quite a lot, what it didn't prepare me for was the amount of "cut-ups" or self harmers I would come across whilst working with female prisoners.

You would have you're general attention seekers who would scratch their skin, then you would have those that would go the whole way. They would slice their skin open with whatever they could find. Usually this would be a razor blade. When I say slice open their skin I do mean cut it open all the way to the bone. Then they would pull the skin apart and in some cases insert objects into the wound. Common examples of this would be batteries, pens and pen re-fills. You always knew the ones that self harmed as they had scars all over their body. I remember asking one youngster why? Why would you want to disfigure yourself in this way. She said it was a way of releasing tension and anger within her body. Once the blood was able to escape, her tension and her anxieties would disappear, at least until the next time, which in reality could be a matter of hours.It then became the job of the nurses to try and re stitch the wound. I say re stitch, because these girls would cut open the wound time and time again. Eventually some wounds just had to be left to heal on there own. Some people say "Oh I couldn't do you're job", and in truth some couldn't. But you got used to seeing people self harm, you get used to clearing away the blood or trying to convince them to hand over the blade. It's part and parcel of prison life. After all you can't just leave them. Although there was one particular officer, who when threatened by the prisoner that she would "cut up" if she didn't get what ever it was that she wanted, would turn around and say "go on then, do it, it's not my body" and not bat an eye lid. The worst part of watching someone cutting up is the feeling of helplessness, because until the prisoner wants to hand over the blade, there is no way you're going to get it of them.

One evening during association, one of our "Young ladies" was mouthing off. She hated everyone. She was becoming "Out of control", so we were ordered to escort her to the segregation unit where she would spend the night. As she was prepared to walk there, we didn't have to use C&R on her, which was good for us. We had just located her in her cell and had began to walk out when she said to our Senior Officer (who by the way was Indian and very proud of it) "You can get out of my face, take you're stinking breath away you fucking lesbian paki". With that Sam turned around, we thought she was going to loose it. She went up to the prisoner, looked her straight in the face and said " ill get out of you're face, my breath may stink, you can call me a lesbian but don't ever call me a paki, I'm Indian". With that she left the cell, slamming the cell door firmly behind her.

Through all its bad points, I never heard a lot a racism at Bullfield. Although it did go on. In the female estate you get more "Keep away from my girlfriend" and that's not only from prisoners but staff as well. If anything staff were intimidated by other staff, especially the new ones, some of the more experienced staff found this to be a good game to play on the new recruits.

When you're a new officer, just out of training, all you want to do is to use your C&R. More commonly known as wrapping people up. Some staff say you get "A buzz". I never did, that "Buzz" never came in 15yrs of service. It was one part of the job that I never enjoyed or even wanted to take part in, although sometimes you had no choice. But there was those that did enjoy it, they did enjoy inflicting pain, Why –Simply because they could.

Twice in 10yrs I've gone for promotion, but instead of failing it twice I decide to tell people that I have found two ways of not passing it. I always felt I was better dealing with prisoners than I was pushing paper. I believed that I could make a difference, no matter how small.

There are some nasty female prisoners around today, who are still in the system after 15yrs; there is equally some nasty staff around as well. It is fair to say that the Prison Service has some excellent members of staff, who are trying to make a difference. But they are few and getting fewer.

The Government every year tells us that we have to manage with less and less money. Our budgets are cut even more. What they don't deal with is that we are getting more and more prisoners, but less and less staff. At Bellfield you could be on your own with 30+ female prisoners, at HMP Sutton it could just be you with 95 male prisoners. Not good odds for you if the S---- hits the fan.

A good governing Governor is hard to find these days. It seems that they are only interested in there bonus and there next promotion. At least the ones that I know are.I would like to acknowledge one Governor at Bellfield, her name was Sue. She genuinely cared about her staff and the prison. She was a credit to the Prison Service and a fantastic Governor.

I spent 4yrs as "Block officer", fighting day in day out. This eventually took its toll on my health and I decided to apply for a transfer. Six months later I was off to HMP Sutton.

Before I left my friends threw me a party at our local pub. One of our Governors came, he was called Geoff, he was another excellent governor. I remember him saying "Girl your going to be so ill in the morning", and boy was he right. But there's one thing prison officers can do and that's party.

I had heard good reports about HMP Sutton and after my weeks leave had finished I was to be on my way. I needed a new challenge, something different and there was nothing more different than going from a female prison to a male prison.

HMP Sutton

I was excited yet nervous about my move to Sutton Prison. Although I had worked with male staff before, I had no experience with male offenders, which is what they had to be called now. This was to be my first of two moves to Sutton. My first three years went well. I had a good rapour with not only the offenders but with my managers as well.

Life certainly had changed for the better. My health had returned and I was enjoying all of the challenges that were being thrown at me. The only difficulty I found in the beginning was getting used to 90+ men walking around in there boxer shorts first thing in the morning, you soon learn to keep eye contact at all costs. There was no fighting, no "wrapping" offenders up, not by be anyway. When an alarm bell did sound, which was not very often, I would be on my toes to the scene. I never wanted to be the last getting there. It was important as a female to be seen to be able to hold your own.Even when the girls did get there first, our male colleagues would hardly ever let us get involved. Even if we tried, the offenders would block our way just in case we got hurt, which was all very nice but we were there to do a job. This was a different kind of respect which at first I found hard to handle and to even understand it.

I learnt very early on in my career not to make promises you cannot keep or have no intension of keeping. The way to earn respect was to keep your promise or else have a dam good reason why you let someone down.

Being based on a wing had its ups and downs. Every so often we would have to do cell searches. You had to do so many per month. Many officers couldn't be bothered with this so they would just sit on the prisoner's bed for 20 minutes watching the T.V. You were supposed to leave the cell in the same condition that you found it, but some officers would trash it, simply because they could get away with it. If we didn't meet our targets we would be told by the wing Senior Officer to sign the book to say that the cell had been searched even when it hadn't. This way he wouldn't get into trouble. This happened on a regular basis at Sutton, especially in the summer when we had the maximum on leave due to holidays. We still had to meet our targets do the "Books were cooked" even more. Nobody seemed to care, everyone knew about it even our managers.

Working on the wing or units was all very well and good, but I needed something different. I self taught myself the "Induction Programme" for when new offenders arrived at the establishment. I soon became the No1 induction officer. The induction course was for two weeks, where they, the offenders got to know me and the system and we, the staff got to know them. We got to know what issues they had – if any and what was needed to rehabilitate them back into society. Every offender that entered Sutton came through me first. Poor sods you might think, but I knew all about them and that earn't me respect.

The majority of offenders called me by my Christian name, I didn't mind this but there was a lot of staff that did. Once they left my unit, technically they were some one else's responsibility, but they used to come back to me when they had a problem even if it was a year later and ask for my help. I always said to them, "If you need to sound off, come and find me", it was better them doing this in front of me than some happy knicking member of staff who didn't give a dam. My opinion was that we all get angry and need to express ourselves, but we can go home, where can they go. Don't get me wrong, I'm no goody goody. I've had my fair share of reporting offenders and wrapping them up but sometimes you just need to take a different approach. That statement was to follow me around Sutton for the Seven years I was there. I always tried to make time to listen, but if I couldn't I would always go and find them later. I found that some staff thought the way that I did but the majority didn't, Why – probably because they just couldn't be bothered. Why give yourself more work when you don't have to. But despite what ever the others thought about the way I worked, we all had one thing in common. We had a duty of care to look after these offenders. This wasn't always easy, especially when you had to deal with some one that was in for child abuse or for beating up some old lady for her pension. We had them all.

New arrival were mostly doubled up (Two to a cell) for there first few days. After which they would get there own cell with a coloured TV, curtains, Duvet, Kettle and an ample supply of tea and coffee. Oh yes and two hot meals a day. Some of the youngsters would complain about there living conditions, but they all got the same reply, which was. Consider yourselves lucky your in prison in this country and as Ronnie Barker out of Porridge put it, if you can't do the time then don't do the crime.

Every prison has stories to tell and Sutton is no exception. I remember one young lad, he was only about 20rs old, he stood out on the induction programme like a sore thumb. Not because he was loud or had a lot to say for himself, which most of them do, but because he said nothing, not a single thing. He remained on my unit for about three months which wasn't unusual. We all noticed the change in him. He became abusive and very angry with himself and life. He never received visits from his family and all he would say is "don't worry I'm not going to be hear for long". I immediately took this to be, he was considering suicide You do learn to pick up and interpret what people say.

I spoke to my S/O (Senior Officer), he was a grumpy old guy, but we got on well. I asked if I could be Jason's personal officer. (Every offender was assigned a personal officer). Mr Smith agreed.

Over the next few weeks, I gained Jason's trust and we spent many hours talking. It turned out that he had been abused by his uncle from an early age, naturally Jason was unable to deal with this, so too block it out he turned to drugs and stealing which eventually lead to his prison sentence. Jason's family were unaware of any of this and because of the shame he bought on his family they had disowned him. One day Jason sought me out and said that he needed his family to know what had happened, but he didn't know how to go about this. We spent many hours discussing it and after consulting my managers we set about contacting his family. Jason's family were shocked to receive a phone call from me, but I persuaded them that they should hear what Jason had to say. They agreed to meet with me first and Jason later. Due to the sensitive nature of the visit, it was agreed that Jason would meet his family away from other offenders. Jason insisted that I sit with him throughout the visit. He had a nice family and they listened to what I had to say. Jason told his family all about what had happened to him during his childhood and why he started to steal and take drugs. Occasionally Jason would turn to me, his eyes were filled with sadness, I knew he wanted me to carry on the conversation, which I did until he was able to continue. There was no way I was going to let this kid down, not now, he had come so far. Jason's family had agreed to support him as long as he remained drug free. They continued to visit him, and as far as I know everything is still ok. Jason, like so many other youngsters in our prisons today just needed someone to believe in them and to help them.

One day I was asked to complete a cell search. My colleague and I entered the cell, it looked like a bomb had gone off in it. There was rubbish ever where. This particular day we had run out of protective gloves to wear. Gloves are worn to protect us from coming into contact with blood or some other unwelcome substances. I decided to go ahead and complete the search without the gloves. I was near the end of the search when I came across a plastic bottle which had been cut in half. Inside the bottle was foam which had been pulled out of the prisoner's pillow. It was arranged so that a whole had been left in the middle of the bottle. A plastic bag had been tied around the out side of the bottle. I couldn't understand what it was that I had found and so being nosy I decided to pull it apart. There was nothing inside it but it was quite sticky. Once the cell search was complete I removed the article, along with a couple more items and took them back to the wing office. It was lunch time when the prisoner came back onto the wing. The wing office was full of prisoners waiting to get their mail. I called the prisoner into the office and informed him that I had completed a search on his cell that morning. I told him that I had taken away certain articles, to which he replied "Ok Miss". I then asked him what the bottle was for, by this time I had picked it up of the desk and was holding it in my hands. He said "It's a sex aid Miss for masturbation, can I have it back". Everyone in the office turned and looked at me. I was lost for words. I didn't know what to do or what to say. In the end I just said "Thank you" and threw it back at him. I thought, how typical, the only time in 13years I didn't wear any gloves and I decide to pull something apart with my fingers. Over the next fortnight all I could hear from the staff was "Here comes sticky fingers". It took me ages to live that one down.

Although Sutton had a lot of "Younger" staff, there was still a lot of staff that thought prison was no place for females to work. That we should be at home looking after our "men" and doing the house work. Some of them took a lot of convincing that we were her to stay and that we could actually do the job as well as they could, sometimes better. Some of our more "Mature" staff still thought they were working back in the 60's and had an attitude to match it. They didn't like change and some just refuse to change. This made it harder to be accepted in what is a dominating male environment.

There are many stories that can be told, but not all have a happy ending. Not everyone will except help and some I'm sorry to say are just beyond helping. But you never give up trying. Despite what the public think or the way in which the prison service is portrayed, were not there just to lock people away, not all of us anyway.

On many occasions, due to staff shortages I would be asked to take charge of my unit, I would become a TSO (Temporary Senior Officer). I enjoyed this and welcomed it at every opportunity. My managers were still insisting I go for promotion but I was still happy just doing my job the best way I knew how.

A year before I transferred again we had a new Governor, his name was Ted- he was great. He was very caring and understanding. I remember he always used to say "Don't bring me a problem; bring me a solution to the problem".

At this point Sutton was beginning to get very bitchy which was surprising coming from the male staff. There was an atmosphere in the air which seemed to last for months. We were short of staff and it seemed to get worse. Evening association for the offenders got cancelled and they would have to stay locked up until the following morning.

By this time I had spent 7yrs with females and 3yrs with males, but now it was time to try something new. I applied for and got a transfer to a prison in the Midlands. It was an "open" prison, which meant no walls, no razor wire.

Two days before I left Sutton, I had this awful feeling that I was about to make the biggest mistake of my life. What did I know about "Open" prisons I thought? Nothing. But knowing me I would soon learn.

Before I left I decided to pay a visit to the Governor. I told him how I was feeling. He said I should do what was right for me, but I didn't know at that time what that was. His parting words were- Jo if it doesn't work out, give me a ring, ill take you back Thanks Ted I really appreciated that. Leaving your friends is always difficult; leaving a prison you loved is even harder.

Where was I

I arrived at a "Mansion" looking building on a cold damp frosty morning, where was I. This couldn't be a prison, there's offenders walking about unescorted, there's no walls, no gates no nothing. I was convinced I had turned up at the wrong place. But No this was it. Oh well, I thought, it couldn't get any worse, could it.

It didn't take long to get used to the routine as there wasn't one. There was no cell checks, no discipline and the offenders were still coming and going as they pleased. I did have an interview with the Governor, I can't remember what was said after he told me "If you feel stressed, get a radio and go for a walk in the grounds". I couldn't believe what I was hearing. Stressed, how could anyone get stressed working here, but it did come and it came like a bolt of lightening. Not because of the work, there wasn't any, and what there was, you could do in about 45minutes. What the hell was I going to do for the other 11hrs and 15mins of my day. My stress came because of the slack attitude by the staff. I always remember one officer, he had been there since he finished his training 14yrs ago. He used to sit in a chair every morning reading a newspaper from front to back, then he would spend another half an hour discussing what was in it. I remember asking him, why he never put in for a transfer. His reply was "Why should I work when I can get paid for doing nothing and have an easy life. As far as I know he is still there. Most days I would take myself off to the woods for a walk. No one ever bothered me or asked me where I had been. The only time I had to be inside the building was for roll check which did happen three times a day. But it was a common event that one offender would decided to have it on his toes. I did work within the so called security dept most days, dealing with the paperwork. Where that was generated from I still don't know. But it kept me busy and I appreciated that.

I was told that the Deputy Governor was an alcoholic, true or not I don't really know. What I do remember is that every time you used to knock on his door, you would hear the clattering of glass. He would then light up his pipe as if he was trying to cover up the smell of whiskey. He never did much and rarely came out of his office, so the drinking never really became an issue for the staff. Except that it is Prison policy that alcohol is not allowed within any establishment, open or closed. Is this one rule for management and another for the staff? Had that been an officer, he or she would certainly have been dismissed from the service for gross misconduct.

I had managed to last six months before I made that hopeful telephone call back to Ted. Ted agreed to take me back as soon as my Governor would let me go. Great I thought 4 maybe 6 weeks I'll be off, after all there was no shortage of staff who wanted to come here and have an easy, quiet life. The Governor, who I had obviously up set decided to keep me the full six months. I have to agree this was my fault at least in part. He asked me why I wanted to leave his prison so soon after getting there. I don't think he appreciated my reply. I should have kept my mouth shut as those six months felt like a life time.

From Heaven
to Hell

A year after I had left HMP Sutton I was back. This is where I belonged. My first year back went well. Two new governor grades had arrived, but sadly Ted had gone. He was going to be missed. We had a couple of "Stand-in" Governors, but they soon left. It was as if I had never been away, nothing had changed. One of our new governor grades was a female. Her name was Sarah McDonald, because she had moved from a prison in the north of England, when she arrived she stayed in what is called the bachelor quarters. They are basically a self contained room whist sharing a toilet, shower room and kitchen. It wasn't ideal. Sarah and I got on well together, she would come round to the house and have a meal or just simply a chat and a bottle of beer. So much so, that we would often go across to France for a day out.

Unfortunately for me this was to be the hardest and most emotional and demanding time of my life.

On January 13th 03, I made the worst mistake of my life. The result of this day would eventually lead to my resignation from the prison service.

It was 20.00hrs, myself and three male colleagues were waiting to leave work for the evening. We were in what is called the "Gate Lodge", it's an area of about 10 x 10ft. When Officer Smith, a long serving member of staff made a racist comment that "All the pakis seem to be leaving the country". Did I just hear what I thought I heard? Even if you think it you certainly don't say it. The comment disturbed me all night, this wasn't the first time I had heard him make racist remarks. I told a friend who said I should report him. My initial thought was "Are you mad"? You don't report fellow officers. It's just not the done thing.

I had decided the best thing to do was to speak to Officer Smith. We went into the wing office. I told him that I found his remark to be offensive and racist. All I wanted him to do was to accept that what he said was wrong and to apologise. Needless to say he refused and told me to stop ear-wigging and to keep my nose out of things. Mr Smith stormed out of the office shouting "The bitch just called me racist".

That evening I was approached by Officer Jones, who was our Union Rep. He asked me if I was going to report Mr Smith. I said "Yes". Mr Jones asked me if I would give him until tomorrow morning so that he could speak with Smith. This wasn't an unfair request so I agreed. After all, the last thing I really wanted to do was to report him, but then you have to ask yourself where do you draw the line. The very next day Mr Jones said that Smith would not take any notice of him, he just wouldn't listen. I sought advice from Sarah as to what I should do. She simply said "If I felt strongly enough about it, then I should make a complaint".

On the 16th January 2003, I made my complaint of Racism against Officer Smith. What made it worse for me was that the officer was white.

Six days later I was informed by my Principle officer that Mr Smith had been suspended from duty – pending an investigation. Strangely enough the very next day my car which had been parked outside my house had been tampered with. Coincidence or not, I don't think so. An investigation did take place; all of the officers that were in the Gate Lodge were questioned. What amazed me even more was the fact that Officer Smith asked S/O Twigg (he was an Asian officer who the comment was made about) if he would supply him with a character reference. S/O Twigg obliged. I asked myself why! Why would you do that. The only answer my friends and I came up with was that he was after promotion and he didn't want to make waves. After all it is hard enough to get promotion if you're white, let alone if you were Asian or from another ethnic background. In the six years I spent at Sutton, we only ever had two ethnic minority members of staff and I was told that one of them resigned because of the way in which he was treated. On the 26th February Officer Smith returned to duty. The report I was given said that it was "possible" that I had misheard what had been said. Surprisingly enough my colleagues never backed me, even though one of them a Mr Bridge, did state to another female officer that he had heard what had been said but because he was still in probation he couldn't say anything and besides which Smith was his friend. It was obvious that my complaint had not gone down well, at least ¾ of the staff refused to talk or to acknowledge me. It was the "good old boys club" and they were sticking together. Even at this early stage I began to feel isolated. But I still had the comforting thought that at least some officers knew that I would not have taken this course of action lightly and they did feel it was about time Mr Smith was brought into line. Even if they were not prepared to do it themselves.

On March 2nd, I was called into the Wing S/O's office, present was Mr Bridge. Mr Bridge had apparently complained to the boss that I was ignoring him. He complained that on one occasion he had asked me if I would like a cup of tea, "No" I replied. Then on another occasion he asked if I wanted a cigarette, as I had only just had one I said "No". Mr Bridge stated that he was having some personal problems and didn't need the stress. I informed both parties that I was not interested in Mr Bridge's problems. After all I was having enough of my own (which he was well aware of as he was one of the officers present when the Racist remark was said) however I would remain professional towards him. With that I turned and left the office. What a bloody cheek..

The 3rd of June was to be the start of many threatening and abusive letter and phone calls that I was going to receive. They ranged from "Where watching you bitch" "You're not safe at work" "You're no better than the scum we lock up". I threw the first letter away, thinking that it would be a one off. At this point I had not informed anyone of the letters, I had brought this on myself and I had to deal with it myself. I didn't know who to trust and who to talk too, I was so alone.

But it was building up inside me and I felt I had nowhere to turn. I kept asking myself why didn't I just ignore him and keep my mouth shut like everyone else. One of the letters made reference to my relationship with Governor McDonald. What relationship I thought. She was a good friend but that was all. Even she had no idea what was happening. Although she did come round one evening and as it happens I was on the phone to a friend in the police force. After my conversation had ended she said "Is there something you want to tell me, you know you can". I said, there was something going on but I didn't want to talk about it. But I so desperately did want to talk about it, all the time she was at my house that night, I kept saying to myself "just tell her, show her the letters", but I didn't want to appear weak or to ask for help so I said nothing, but I was grateful for her concern. I was now receiving internal phone calls, mainly just "grunts and groans". These carried on for months. Every day I would walk into the Prison, not knowing what to expect.

One particular day I was walking up the stairwell on my unit, when an offender stopped me. He said "I need to speak to you miss". "sorry" I said "I'm busy at the moment, catch me later". "I know what's happened" he said. I stopped and turned towards him. "What's happened" I said. " I know miss, I know". "What do you know Andy"? "I know about you and Smith and the letters". My face must have said a thousand things. Andy had certainly got my attention. "Don't believe all you hear Andy" I said, and I turned to walk away. "Were not having it" Andy shouted at me. I stopped and turned towards Andy again. "Whatever you think you know, your mistaken" I said. "Then why were two officers talking about it on the landing last night". Andy told me who the two officers were. "We will sort him" Andy said. I told Andy to leave well alone, it had all been sorted out. It was almost a relieve to know someone was on my side even though it was a prisoner. That evening I spoke with Mr Jones, who was apparently one of the officers, talking about it. Mr Jones confirmed that he was talking about what had happened but not on the landing. Wherever it was, Andy certainly knew the facts.

The following day was my "Rest day". It was two days later when I heard that Mr Smith had had a bucket of urine and vomit thrown over him in his wing office. He didn't know who had done it. At this point I made no connection with my conversation with Andy. Mr Smith wasn't liked by the prisoners and there was always someone threatening to get him. There was nothing that Mr Smith liked more than to wind up the prisoners, to be offensive. We all heard it over the years but unfortunately he wasn't the only one.

Several weeks later, Mr Smith was on duty standing on the ground floor of "B" wing, with his back to the wing door. It was association time, so the prisoners were coming and going as usual. All of a sudden the alarm bell sounded. Apparently a prisoner had come up behind Mr Smith and given him a severe beating. I heard he ended up with a broken jaw and ribs. It was general opinion that this was an assault waiting to happen. As far as I was concerned Smith was making my life hell and had turned the staff against me, (some of them follow like sheep). So I wasn't going to loose any sleep over this attack on him I'm sorry to say. The prisoner, when questioned on why he did it said it was to repay a drugs debt. It must have been one hell of a debt, as the prisoner was on three strikes and out. (This meant that another offence committed and he would be serving a life sentence). The prisoner was shipped out the next day and I heard nothing more about him.

I sought out Andy, after hearing of what had happened to Smith. I took him into the wing office. "Well" I said, "What was that all about".

"Don't worry miss, it had nothing to do with you"

"It had better not" I replied or I will drag you in front of the Governor.

Whether or not these two assaults on Smith were coincidental or not I don't know.

It was strange though, I felt safer around the prisoners than I did around my own colleagues and my so called friends. For many weeks I stayed close to my unit, only going off when it was absolutely necessary. I became aware that I was being watched, guarded if you like, but not by the staff but by the prisoners. I felt safe whilst they were around.

During the month of July, a letter had been sent to Sarah, stating that I was having an affair with a prisoner on "D" wing. When I questioned this, I was informed that the letter had not been taken seriously and nothing further would happen. I was not happy with this, someone was trying to tarnish my name and I wanted it investigated, after all I had nothing to hide. A month had gone by and still no investigation, in the end I gave up. I suppose I should have been grateful to the Governor and management that they knew I could not and would not do anything that would bring me before a disciplinary board.

August 29th became the final straw, after yet another letter stating that "No one knows who we are". I felt sick; this wasn't going to go away. I decided to tell the duty Governor, who happened to be Jo Carr. She was an excellent Governor who had come up through the ranks and was well respected. It was a Saturday, I asked if I could speak with her "off the record" before we unlocked the prison for afternoon association. Jo came to the wing almost straight away and we went into her office. I showed Jo the letters I had received and the diary I had kept. I had written down everything that had happened and what had been said. Within five minutes I was in absolute tears. Jo said although she would not push me on it, but I should bring this all out into the open and have it investigated. She asked if I had spoken to Sarah about it. I said that I hadn't but she was aware that something had been going on. I became so distressed that Jo sent me home. Jo had contacted Sarah and asked her if she could meet her at my house, she briefly informed Sarah of what had happened. By the time both Sarah and Jo arrived at my house I was still distressed and had been drinking heavily. I remember it was a hot summer's day, but I felt very cold and was shaking badly. Jo stayed with me for a couple of hours, but had to return to the prison as she was the Duty Governor. Sarah stayed well into the evening. She asked why I hadn't told her what had been going on. It's not as if I never had the opportunity. The simple fact was that I didn't know how to. I was to o ashamed to admit that this was happening to me. For the first time in my life I couldn't handle what was happening to me. I agreed that the police should be contacted and I gave my statement. The police didn't really seem to take much interest in the case. I had given them a few weeks to make there inquiries and had heard nothing back. When I phoned them to find out what was happening I was informed that the case would remain open but there was a lack of evidence to go on and the investigation had ceased. I was amazed that nobody had had the decency to inform me. Another investigation was to take place but nothing ever came of it as the phone calls and letters had stopped and the prison didn't want to stir up more trouble and make things worse. How could things get any worse I thought, but they did. I just didn't know it at the time. Due to stress and depression I spent a period of time away from work. My doctor (who knew everything that was going on by this time) prescribed me anti-depressants, I couldn't even face going to our local supermarket just in case I bumped into one of them. On a few occasions I saw a couple of them in my village. They never said anything, they just stared me out like it was a cool thing to do. I got to the point where I wouldn't leave the house, then I got angry because I had been made a prisoner within my own home. It took all of my strength to pick up a friend from the train station at times. I was only comfortable when I had locked myself in for the evening. I wouldn't even answer the telephone. Sutton had a new Governor in place by the time I returned to work, his name was Mr Dickinson. He was well known in the prison system for getting what he wanted. On my return I was due to work on the other side of the prison on "D" wing. But it wasn't long before another letter had arrived stating "I wasn't welcome on the west side". I decided to ask the new Governor for another investigation as I believed the first two were flawed. Mr Dickinson replied, stating that he had looked into the case and he was not prepared to order another investigation, however he did offer me a transfer, but at my own expense. I couldn't afford this, so I had to decline and stay where I was. It was obvious I was becoming a problem and no-one wanted me around. Especially as I was taking the prison service and in particular HMP Sutton to an Industrial Tribunal over harassment and failing to protect me whilst on duty.

On Aug 14th I had another period of work due to Stress and depression. I had taken my sick note into the prison that morning, but by mid afternoon my line manager had phoned me to ask when would I becoming back to work. Not how are you, can we do anything for you..Nothing. On the 30th, David our Head of Personnel phoned me to see how I was, this surprised me. In 14yrs I have never had the H.O.P phone me to ask how I was feeling.

I thought my luck was beginning to change when on the 4th Aug I had been informed that I could transfer to a prison nearby. I had spoken to the Governor there and he agreed that I could start the week after my Tribunal had ended. I truly began to believe that life was changing for the better. A new start and a new Prison. I was sad but happy and relieved to be leaving Sutton prison.

The 7th of Aug was party night. It's a party that has been held every year at my house and I didn't see why this year should be any different. Sarah Mcdonald came round, she never really spoke that much to me all evening, and she asked how I was. I said that I felt like I was being forced to leave Sutton. Upon leaving she said she would be in contact next week and we would meet up. I never saw her again until July 05. I know she had been told to stay away, she even admitted it to a friend.

For many months afterwards I blamed her for abandoning me, for letting me cope alone. It's only now that I realise and appreciate what pressure had been placed on her, after all she had her own career to think about as well.

On the 16th of August, was to have been my day in court, my day, to say what I heard all those months ago and how I had been treated since. I was sat outside the court room when a funny old man came up to me and asked "What do you want to swear on" I looked at my barrister, I had know idea what this guy was going on about. It turned out that he was the court clerk and he wanted to know if I was going to swear on the bible or something else. I said that the bible would be fine. Within a few minutes both sets of barristers were sat in a corner talking. I remained outside the court room with my friend whom I had taken along for support. My barrister came back and said that we needed to talk. He said that as soon as I am asked if I am prepared to tell the truth the whole truth and nothing but the truth and I reply yes then I will have committed perjury and that I could loose my job. I didn't understand this at all. The barristers got me so worked up that I didn't know if I was coming or going. They kept saying I'm going to loose. How did they know that, I hadn't even got inside the court yet? I was so distressed I walked out of the court and away from the tribunal. God only knows how I got home that day.

That afternoon I was informed that I had to report to the prison as the Governor wanted to see me. He informed me that the police would be re-investigating the case. Great I thought, why the hell didn't you do this months ago when I asked for it. It turned out that the police would now be investigating ME. I was also informed that my transfer would be suspended until the outcome of the police investigation. I thought there's no way I'm going back into Sutton, so I remain off work. I was also informed that as soon as I reported fir for duty the Governor would call me in and suspend me from duty until the investigation had run its course. Low and behold as soon as I reported fit for duty I was suspended. Investigations, suspension, this was all new to me. I kept being told "Do this, do that, don't let them know about this or that". Little did I know I was continuously given bad advice by my union representatives. But they knew best or so I thought. By the time evening had come my head was spinning. I was trying to make sense of everything that had happened.

It turns out that I was being investigated on the grounds that I possibly wrote the letters to myself and made phone calls to myself. I don't know quite how I managed the phone calls !!

When I asked my union rep of the possible outcome, all they kept saying was that I would be dismissed from the Prison service on the grounds of possibility. I couldn't believe what I was hearing.

My family knew nothing of what had been going on over the past few months. I would hate to think what they would have said if they did.

On the 24th Aug, DS Nickson came to the house to see me. I was expecting a call at some stage so this was not too much of a shock. What came as a shock was the fact that he gave me what he called the "chance to come clean". Come clean about what I said I have done nothing wrong. But then I thought, "No, you have done something wrong. You made a complaint about a white officer making a Racist remark. That's what you've done wrong girl". So yes I am guilty for standing up for what I believed in and the system I believed in. How stupid could I have been? I told DS Nickson to carry on with his investigation, do what he needed to do as I had nothing to hide.

I remember meeting up with Gov Ted in our staff social club, we talked a lot about what had happened. All he said to me was "You won't win girl". How right you were.

I was contacted by a member from the RESPECT organisation. (Racial Equality for Staff and Prisoners Trust). They wanted my permission to write to the Director General, Phil Wheatley and to the Area Manager. I said if you think it's going to do any good then go ahead. I never did hear anything more from them. Everybody seemed to want to get involved but in fact nobody did anything. Why are we funding a "Trust" that does nothing for its members, that will not tackle issues of Racism. Is it not why they are their. If their not going to help staff than do you honestly believe there going to help a prisoner.

In the months that followed I voluntarily gave samples of my own handwriting and DNA. I thought why not, I still had nothing to hide and it might speed things up a bit. In October 04, the police informed me that my handwriting samples that I had given were not consistent with the letters that I had received. (I could have told them that months ago). Equally the samples given by the other men that I suspected, who were also being tested was not consistent. The police concluded that no further action would be taken. I thought, at least now I can go on my transfer and put all of this behind me.

Nothing happened for four days, No contact by the prison, all I was waiting for was for the Governor to call me in and lift my suspension and let me get on my way. Somehow I should have known better, on the 4th Nov a DS Morris knocked on my door. She asked if she could speak to me, so we sat in my lounge. I had know idea what she wanted but I soon found out. She said "In light of new evidence the case was to be re-opened" "New evidence, what new evidence" I said. It turns out that the Governor was not happy with the outcome of the police investigation and so he had sought out a letter I had written back in 1996 to the Head of Personnel, where the capital T looks the same as the capital T in the letters that I received. I couldn't believe what I was hearing. It was now evident that the Governor now had a personal vendetta out against me. This became more obvious when the union rep told me of a conversation he had had with the Governor, where Mr Dickson openly admitted that he knew I was guilty. I phoned the prison and asked to speak with Mr Dickinson. I asked him where this memo came from, he told me that the police had requested it. I told Mr Dickson that the police state that he gave it to them. I remember his voice becoming very aggressive and he had the cheek to tell me he didn't like my attitude.

I could never understand why Mr Dickinson had such a personal grudge against me. It was not only clear to me but to two Governor Grades that I stayed in contact with that he did have a grudge and that this was becoming personal with him. Everyone said I was being harassed and intimidated by him. Only later would I realise what the "Grudge" was all about. Unfortunately this has to remain a secret and is not for print as I fear this would jeopardise yet another career.

On Wed 15th December, Sgt Doyle phoned me, he said he wanted to speak to me and could I attend the police station. At the time I thought it was a little strange that he didn't ask if he could come round to the house, but thought nothing more of it. We agreed that I would attend the police station the next afternoon. The next day Sgt Doyle and a WPC who I had not met before met me inside the lobby of the station. We walked through a secure door, and then Sgt Doyle began to read out something from his note pad. By the time I realised what was happening, he had finished reading his statement which was, that I was being arrested for attempting to pervert the course of justice, by writing letters and making phone calls to myself. I couldn't believe what I was hearing. I was escorted down to the custody sergeants desk there stood four officers. The custody sergeant listened to the charge and then asked me for my name and occupation. As soon as I said Prison Officer, everyone turned and looked at me. The Sgt asked if I would like a solicitor, I replied "Do I need one". She said it was up to me but I could request one later if I wished. I declined the offer. I was lead into a small dirty little office, I sat one side of the table and the Sgt and the WPC sat the other side. One of them then proceeded to switch on the tape machine. They then began to ask me a series of questions, over and over again. Did I write the letters myself, I replied "No". Had I seen these letters before, I thought of course I have you idiot, it was me that gave them to you. After what seemed like a life time the Sqt switched the machine off. I thought now what's happening. Ths Sgt then told me that there was not enough evidence to proceed and that I was free to go. I cannot begin to describe what it was like to be arrested. How can people commit a crime and go through this time after time. The Sgt told me that Mr Dickinson had been informed that I was going to be arrested. He continued to say that they would be contacting him again once I had left the station to inform him of the out come. How disappointed he must have been to receive a phone call saying that they were not proceeding with the case and I had not been charged. That must have really pissed him off. That afternoon I was due to collect a friend from the station, because I had been held at the police station I was late collecting her. She had made her way home. She phoned me and asked "Where had I been". I told her what had happened that afternoon. I remember saying to her "When is this all going to end". It was a very traumatic experience being arrested, not one I believe any innocent person would ever put themselves through.

I had decided to tell my mother and family what had been happening. I was running out of excuses as to why I wasn't at work. They were shocked to say the least. My mother, god bless her wanted to go and "Sort him out". I don't know quite what she had in mind as she's only 5'1". But she would have tried given the chance. She couldn't as I couldn't understand why the Service had turned its back on me, when all I did was to report an incident in which the service has a zero tolerance policy.

During the whole ordeal from Jan 03 to the present day, there have been three Governor Grades that have stuck by me. They have given me advice, for which I have always been grateful. I asked them all once, Why, why do you believe me and no one else does. "Its simple", they said, "We know you". That was good enough for me.

After being released by the police, I'm still waiting for Mr Dickinson to call me into the prison to lift my suspension. Wrong, Why did I think it was all over? You would have thought that I would have known better, especially where Mr Dickinson was concerned.

The next day I received a phone call from my union rep saying that the prison service would be conducting yet another investigation. I thought God this has got to come to an end soon. I had lost all respect for the prison service and my Governor.

I was told that the investigation would be conducted by two Senior Officers from Sutton

Prison. These officers had worked for Mr Dickinson before at there last establishment. They were "Yes" men and were keen to "Get on" in the service, so there was no way that they were not going to find me guilty and go against Dickinson. I spoke to a friend, I couldn't take anymore. I was now at the lowest point that I had ever been in my life. I sat at a table with a bottle of tablets and a bottle of whiskey. I could see no end to it. I just wanted to get on with my life and my job, but they were not going to allow me to do this. It would have been so easy to end it all. What changed my mind, I really don't know. Maybe it was the thought that someone would have to find me. What would it do to my family? Maybe it was the fact that I didn't want to give Dickinson the satisfaction. Throughout the last month I had applied for jobs, just in case the worst came to the worst. But as soon as I mentioned the prison service and what had gone on, they didn't want to know. That is apart from my present employer. I had been called forward for an interview. I wasn't expecting much especially after my previous attempts at trying to find employment. But a week later I was informed that the main manager would like to interview me. I thought maybe, maybe this is looking good. But I wasn't going to get my hopes up. The process was delayed due to Christmas, but in January, I received a phone call. I remember I was at my auntie's house. I was told that I had got the job and when could I start. I didn't know what to say as it came as a shock and a surprise. I walked into the kitchen, my auntie was stood at the kitchen sink washing up some pots. I said "I've got it, I've got the job". Pauline had tears in her eyes, she was so pleased. Someone other than my family and friends had faith in me and I couldn't wait to start work.

Even today I couldn't describe my emotional state of mind.

On the 21st Dec, nearly two years on, the Governor informed me that my suspension would continue, pending the out come of the investigation. I really was so sick of hearing that, that I really didn't care anymore.

Every Wednesday since I had originally been suspended, I had to phone into the prison at 09.30hrs. One particular day, she wasn't there and the Governor answered. Did I expect him to say anything, No not really, all I got was

"Right thank you". The next time I phoned in, the secretary answering machine was on. I left a message saying "That I was disgusted by the way that I had been treated by the prison service and by my managers. That no one had been in contact with me since my suspension back in Aug". It is Home Office policy that your line manager at least should be in contact with you at least once a week. I received no reply that day. I was asked to report to Sutton on the 14th Jan 05, for the start of the new investigation. I had my union rep with me but they weren't a lot of good. The interview took all of 20minutes. I thought my god, this is going to decide my future and it's only taken 20 minutes. What did I really expect? When it concluded the Senior Officer said something about support. "Support I thought". I saw red and let rip. They wouldn't know what support is if it came up and bit them on the arse. I left and went home. What a surprise at 3.00pm that afternoon my line manager phoned me at home. He said he was un aware that he was still my line manager and assumed that I had transferred. I didn't believe that, did he really think I was that stupid. I told him I didn't need his support and put the phone down. I coped on my own for the past year without any support from Sutton and I will continue to cope on my own. I was so angry.

A month before, I had written to the Area Manager, stating how I had been treated and what was going on and how I believed that Dickinson now had a personal vendetta out against me. It was the middle of January when the Area Managers side kick phoned me and asked if he could meet me. "Great" I thought, now were going to get somewhere. But all it seemed he wanted to know was, was I going to do anything about what had gone on, was I going to tell the newspapers about it, was I going to pursue another court case?

The investigation soon ran its course and it was then handed over to the Governor who I was supposed to be working for when I transferred to my new establishment. I did go and see this Governor and try to put my side across. I truly believed that after reading all of the evidence, the fact that twice I have been cleared by the police and the report I had given him about my own hand writing specialist, that my name would be cleared. I kept saying to people, Why would I write letters to myself in my own handwriting and not typed, knowing that I would supply samples of my own handwriting to the police. What did I have to gain? Money, you might say, but this was never about money. After all I had been offered £10000.00 by the Prison Service to move. Which I declined. I had been offered another transfer which I accepted at my own expense, so where was I going to benefit. All I wanted was an apology, an apology for realising what some one said was offensive and racist, which had it been forthcoming either from Mr Smith or from the Prison service, none of this would have happened.

A couple of weeks later I received a letter from the Governor stating that he had read all the evidence, (but did not take into account the hand writing specialist report) and that I would be dismissed from the Prison Service on the grounds of Possibility. How did I know that was coming? I have always believed that it was better to resign than to be dismissed. I did have the choice to appeal this decision, but I was convinced that this would only prolong the inevitable. The next day I wrote out my letter of resignation. What else could I do? I had served the Prison service for 15yrs and not received so much as a "please explain." I was left feeling absolutely gutted.

I never told my family half of what had happened and for that I apologise, but I was too ashamed to admit that I couldn't handle what had been going on.

All I can say is that Dickinson succeeded in "Getting me out", I hope he is happy with that thought, but it doesn't get away from the problem that he still has someone in his prison that is Racist. Also that Racism, Harassment and Bulling exist inside HMP Sutton.

Some months later I had heard that Sarah McDonald had resigned from the Prison Service. She had been at Sutton for 3yrs or so. She had four or five years to go before retiring. You have to ask yourself why?. Why retire so early. I know some of what happened, but that's another story and probably not mine to tell, but I know it had something to do with Dickinson.

Too the staff, I would say only this "Don't go crying to anyone when it happens to you, because no one will listen".

Too the Home Office. One day you will have to admit that Racism, Bulling and harassment exists within your prisons and its getting worse not better.

Too all existing offenders, Think twice before making a complaint. Although they can't sack you, they can and will make your life hell. You know it, and I've seen it. If you do stand up for your rights to be treated as individuals despite your ethnic back ground then I wish you all the best. I tried but failed.

Prisons today have become more and more about figures and meeting targets, rather than about trying to educate offenders into leading law abiding life's once they have been released. So many times we have seen Governors stop vital classes such as drug awareness courses or counselling classes because they don't have they money. But they always seem to find extra money for conferences or character building sessions or away days. It's never spent where it's needed and it's needed inside our prisons.

I have often wondered what the prisoners have made of all of this. I'm sure they know what has happened. After all no one just goes without something being said. As long as the truth was told, that is my main concern. As for me, well I'm doing rather well now. I work for an international company. I have a great boss and I look forward every day to going to work. I told them at my interview why I had resigned from the Service. It didn't faze them, they let me get on and prove myself and I don't think ive done to bad a job. To my bosses I would like to say thank you for giving me back my self respect and dignity and for giving me a chance. I owe you so much.

A friend once said to me "What goes around comes around". I'm still waiting, but I know my day will come.

The End

Authors Notes

This is a book of tears and laughter, devastation and hope.

This book is not meant to be used as a reprisal or to be vindictive, but simply as a transcript of what transpired in my life and a lesson learned.

All the names in this book have been changed in order to protect the dignity and privacy of others.

This book has been written after much heart ache and sole searching. It depicts the prison Service through the eyes of only one, but the understanding and acknowledgment of many.

This isn't about financial reward, it's about me and having the chance to "Have my say", which was always denied to me by the Prison Service. If I only sell one copy then it will have been worth it.

Chloe, a dear friend said "Be careful of what might be considered as official secret, you know what the service is like, they'll come after you".Well come on, if you're really that stupid. Then let's have the rest of it out in the open, after all I lost everything once, I can loose it again. I have nothing to loose.

Finally to Author house publications, thank you for giving me this chance.

A friend once said "Be brave and the rest will follow".

About the
Author

I was born in 1964, in a small market Town on the east coast of Lincolnshire. I had a very happy and well loved upbringing. From an early age my parents installed in me, love, Honesty and Integrity.

I left school at 17, I had many local jobs such as veterinary nurse, Quilt Inspector and shop assistant to a Pharmacy and local estate agent.

I joined The Women's Royal Army Corp aged 23, it was the best experience of my life. I was due to leave in 1990 and had to get another job, I saw a notice in the local paper, to become a Prison Officer, I applied and was accepted. This is where my story begins.